A Pizza My Life

Surviving the Pizza Industry

George D. Taylor

New Idea Publishing

Taylor, George, 11/12/1963-

A pizza my life: surviving the pizza industry / George D. Taylor – First Edition

Editor: Liz Barrett Foster (lizbarrettfoster.com)

Publisher: New Idea Publishing (newideapublishing.com)

ISBN: Print: 978-1-7329952-1-5 | eBook: 978-1-7329952-2-2

For my parents, James M. Taylor and Julia C. Taylor, and my

wife, Patricia (Patti) M. Taylor.

They have always supported me in every way.

My parents were always there for guidance and assurance. In

our first shop, they would come and sit at the front table on

Friday nights and have dinner.

My wife is my rock.

She has lived this pizza life with me every step of the way.

I could not be where I am today without her.

She's the hardest-working, most amazing woman I've ever

known.

Praise for A Pizza My Life

"George's passion for the pizza industry comes through on the pages of this book. His desire to learn and get better at every step is honestly displayed throughout. Whether you're new to the industry or have been in for decades, there's a story for you in this well-crafted piece of work."

--Nick Bogacz, author of *The Pizza Equation* and president/founder, Caliente Pizza & Draft House

"It's rare to find open and honest conversation about failure in the restaurant industry. George's willingness to share the details and causes of his biggest business mistakes is a breath of fresh air and will help any new or seasoned pizzeria operator who may be feeling alone in their struggles."

--Liz Barrett Foster, former editor-in-chief of *PMQ Pizza Magazine* and author of *Pizza: A Slice of American History*

"George Taylor's, *A Pizza My Life* is a riveting blend of a hard-earned success story and a trench marketing playbook. As George shares his tale, he's able to include you through his emotional journey, both positive and trying, and quite often with a humorous spin. As an example, the book's title, *A Pizza My Life*, funny, yes? Layered into the tale of George's three previous locations and his current successful restaurant, coupled with his trial-and-error method of constantly learning win-win strategies—a learning arises. This is a guidebook for growing a business in the hospitality industry. I love the operational slant. George includes statistics when he shares successes, adding credibility to his thesis. I absolutely agree and applaud his slant on door hangers, employee development, building maintenance, direct mail, POS systems, *not* discounting, inactive customer marketing, consistency of product, public relations, and simply smiling. There are many more hints that will guide you toward success, but you'll have to read George's book cover to cover to enjoy his masterpiece of an end product."

--Rudolf J. Waldner, author of *Marketing from the Trenches* and *The Corporate Jungle*

"Pizza man, family man, and now author. *A Pizza My Life* is an educational tale for both current pizza operators and hopeful pizzaioli alike. Less a cautionary tale and more a chronicling of the difficulties of starting and running a family-owned pizzeria today, George details the hidden pitfalls of pizzeria ownership and the joy of seeing your name on the sign, all culminating in a very positive message for the industry as a whole. A must read for anyone trying to get their slice of the pizza market."

--Brian Hernandez, PMQ test chef/US Pizza Team director

Contents

Introduction

I decided to write this book for several reasons:

1. To give readers a glimpse into what it's like living the pizza life.

2. To talk about my mistakes along the way. There are countless books about how to succeed in the pizza industry. This book will describe, in detail, how and why our business failed, and then how we started over and did it right.

3. After being in the trenches for 25 years, I wanted to tell my story.

Hopefully, through reading this book, you can avoid the mistakes I made. I'm not promising you a ton of revolutionary information that will propel your sales to the next level, but I will tell you how I survived the difficulties of running a pizzeria in America. Everyone's story is different.

Starting a new pizza shop can be filled with long days and sleepless nights. It's your baby. It takes nurturing and attention. If you don't give it what it needs, someone else might come along and steal your customers, or worse, someone on the inside might just steal from *you*.

With all that it takes and demands from you, pizza is still a great business to be in, and I can't imagine many things that I would rather do. If you're reading this, you may feel the same.

I'm not here to burst your bubble about owning a pizzeria. But, because I believe that owning a pizzeria—or any restaurant—is difficult, I've chosen to share what others seldom do. Instead of talking about the good days, I'm going to first talk about what we did wrong in the business. Why? Because I want you to avoid making the same mistakes I did.

Then, I'll take you back to the beginning and tell you a little about how and why I got into the business, where we are today, and share some advice for those interested in starting their own pizza life.

This is my story; I hope you enjoy it and find value in it.

Chapter One

What Went Wrong

There are so many decisions that can take you in one direction or the other. When the end came, I felt like I had failed. We had some good times. We even did well at times. But in the end, our mistakes caught up to us.

Even though we were able to survive in the pizza industry for nearly 20 years, it was sometimes just that—surviving.

Without several cash infusions from my parents and Patti's mom over the years, the end would have found us much sooner. These are the things that keep you up at night.

Patti and I entered the pizza industry on our own in 1995. By 2014, we decided that our shop had run its course, and it was time to close the doors for good.

I've chosen to focus on this time in my pizza life first because there isn't a lot of talk about failure nowadays.

You can find all kinds of books detailing how to run a business and what makes a business successful, but very little content is available about why, and how, businesses fail. It's easy to see why. Failure is hard to admit.

We made a lot of mistakes over the years. Some were minor and didn't have an immediate impact on sales while others were big and affected the top line.

The biggest mistake was probably our failure to draw out a plan before we opened our pizzeria.

I used to justify it by saying that everything happened very quickly in the beginning. When my friend came to me with the proposal of taking over a failing pizza shop, the first thing we should have done was write out a formal plan. Not doing this was a mistake.

We had no idea what our direction was going to be. We were flying by the seat of our pants. Writing a plan helps you have a path to follow toward success. We recognized this early on and still didn't address it.

We're all going to make mistakes, probably several. I'm not saying that by making these mistakes you're not going to make it or that you'll go under if you commit these same errors.

However, if you make enough of them, it will increase the chances that you will struggle, and you may be forced to reconsider if you're in the right business.

I'm going to walk you through some of the mistakes that we made and explain why they were mistakes. Some of them are obvious and after reading them you might wonder what in the world I was thinking. Believe me, I ask myself all the time.

For example, when we bought our first pizza shop, we told the previous owner that we didn't need her recipes. In hindsight, it would have been a good idea to know how to make pizza.

Undercapitalization

I would guess that undercapitalization is probably the biggest thing that we, and many other failed restaurants, have in common. When we opened our restaurant, we had no money.

We purchased the pizzeria using owner financing. The previous owner held a note. We made monthly payments to her for the first three years. We even had to pay the real estate commission the same way and borrowed some money from my parents to make the down payment.

In the first year of business, Patti was still working a full-time job, at a local credit union. Without the income from her job, we never would have made it out of the first year. She paid the bills and put what was leftover into the business. Along with the money, she also came into work when she was done with her day job and would often work into the early hours of the morning.

Even as we started to grow sales, there were several times, throughout our time in the business, that we needed to borrow money from my parents and/or Patti's mother. Sometimes we would have a piece of equipment break, and we didn't have the money to fix it, or we needed to replace something altogether.

The point is, we were lucky to have backup family that were willing to help us out. Without that financial help, we never would have made it as long as we did.

When you get into business for yourself, financial planning must be a big part of the start of your business.

Let's face it. If a person had unlimited funds, it would be easy to keep a business going. It doesn't mean that it would be producing revenue that would grow and create wealth, but you could keep the doors open as long as you wanted.

Be sure to plan for things. Try to be ready for equipment purchases and repairs, inventory, marketing, and day-to-day expenses like rent, utilities, and payroll. As I stated previously, we had no plan. We were winging it all the way and had no business getting into business the way we did.

The Food

Not having a plan may have been a bit of an understatement. Not only did we not have a formal business plan, but we didn't even have a pizza recipe. I had worked at Domino's as a delivery driver for a while before we got into it and occasionally put a pie together. That was it. We had no clue how to make dough or sauce. We didn't even know what cheese to use.

You often hear people with great food recipes talking about how they should get into the restaurant business. They have a sauce recipe that was handed down from their great-great-grandmother from Italy. That was not me. I had nothing.

In the weeks leading up to our opening, we picked a sauce, in a can, that we thought would be good if we added a little sugar to it. The dough was made at a local bakery and dropped off in the morning. The baker had a key and would open the front door and set it just inside. When I would come in several hours later, the dough, which was in bags, was always fully blown. By the way, that was OK because I didn't even know there was such a thing as blown dough.

During the first year we realized it would be a good idea to figure out what we were doing and learn how to make our dough and sauce.

The Name and Logo

We came up with the name Freschott Pizza as a play on the words Fresh Hot Pizza. When answering the phones, it sounded like we were saying, "Thank you for calling Fresh Hot Pizza."

The way we spelled Freschott Pizza was, as you might have guessed, confusing to customers. They didn't get it. For years they mispronounced it due to the way we spelled it. We should have run it by a focus group before running with it.

By focus group, I simply mean showing the name to family and friends, without explaining it first, and seeing if they get it. Ask them, "Does this work?"

Our first logo was simple. It was done as a circle to represent a pizza. The top half of the circle said Freschott and the bottom said Pizza. In the center were the words "Is Fresh Hot Pizza," to explain the name. Then we felt it needed something.

We changed it to a stock graphic of a waiter running with a meal. We changed the meal to a pizza box and added a baseball cap. After using that logo for about a year, we saw another local pizza shop using the same graphic. We needed to make another logo change.

We needed something that represented only us that people could identify with Freschott Pizza. I drew a chef holding a pizza (I'm not bad at drawing) and we finally had something that represented who we were. Unfortunately, it took us between three and four years to get that right.

Between having a name that people didn't understand how to pronounce and a logo that changed three times in the first four years, it was difficult to build a brand. If you're starting a business, be sure to think about these things before you open your doors. I'm not saying that every business has to have a full-blown plan with all of the answers but having a name that people can pronounce easily and a logo that helps identify you certainly makes branding your business an easier task and increases your chance of success.

Use The KISS (Keep It Simple Stupid) method often in business. Making something simple seems like an easy decision, but often we overthink things or try to be too clever or cute and end up missing the mark. This goes for the name and logo. The name should be short and easy to say and remember. The logo should be something that's easily recognized and slightly smaller than a business card in dimensions to use on all of your publications.

Moving

When we bought our first place, we had no idea that we would be moving from that location in just three years. When we signed our lease, it was only for three years and had no renewal option. We were new to this game and just didn't know the rules. We didn't think too far beyond getting the place open.

Unfortunately, when you move, there will be a large number of your customers who think you have gone out of business. Why wouldn't they? The spot that you were in is either vacant now or occupied by someone else. If you're lucky, another pizza shop won't move into your old place to start feeding off your old customer base.

We certainly were not savvy enough to start alerting our customers that we were moving long before it happened. We did keep our phone number and thought everyone would just keep calling. Remember, this was before social media, too. We didn't have Facebook to help us let people know that we were still open but just in a new location.

Part of the problem was that we didn't just move a block or two away. We moved to the adjoining city. When we moved the second time, we moved back to the original city. If you're out of sight, you're out of mind. We had several customers, who eventually found out we moved, tell us that they thought we went out of business.

When you open a business, it's important to understand the details of how you're going to keep it going. The first detail is making sure that you have a place to operate. I assume that when you open a business, the plan is to be in business for a long time. That needs to factor into your lease. It's probably going to take years to build that business to where you want it to be, so it makes sense to have a lease that accommodates that vision. I would suggest a five-year lease with an option for at least another five.

It's also important to give yourself a way out in case things don't work out for one reason or another. Sometimes things happen that you have no control over that hurt your ability to conduct business. For example, when the town decides on a yearlong road improvement project that runs in front of your store, it may leave customers with limited or no access to your business for extended periods of time.

Of course, one way to make sure you always have control over your facility is to purchase the building you intend to house your business in. This is what we finally did. Unfortunately, that meant moving again. That was two moves in the first six years.

It felt like we were starting over. After all, when we moved the first time, some customers saw we weren't where we were, and just assumed we went out of business. We had what we thought would be a good location where we could finally start to build our business without interruption. We had low overhead, a building that we owned, and a newly built restaurant. What could go wrong?

Parking

The first two locations we were in had plenty of parking. It wasn't something that we thought much about because there were enough spots to accommodate any traffic we might have.

However, when we moved to the location we purchased, parking was an issue. The funny thing though is that it wasn't a real problem, it was more of a perceived problem. Perception is reality, or so they say. The Main St. location had on-street parking up and down the street and there was a municipal lot behind the store. However, we didn't have a rear entrance for the public, so customers had to walk around to the front.

Customers often complained that there was nowhere to park. What they meant though, was that there were no spots where they wouldn't have to parallel park or need to walk around half the block from the parking lot. This was a real issue for customers, especially later on as other businesses moved out of the area and people felt less safe if they couldn't park right in front of the store.

I understand the concerns; I just underestimated them. Going forward I will always make sure that parking is ample and well lit.

Inconsistency

Customers want consistency. They want to know what they are getting, where they are getting it from, and when they can get it. Unfortunately, I violated all of these at one time or another and in the end, I believe it was one of the things that ultimately led to decreased sales.

To begin with, we had changed our recipe several times over the years. We were always looking to make a better pizza.

What is better though?

Our customers already liked what we had and that's why they came to our pizza shop. Some of the changes were very subtle and no one even really noticed. Other times people would notice and say it was better.

How many people noticed and didn't care for it?

We will never know.

Then there were the constant changes in menu items. I believe you have to get rid of things if they don't sell. It doesn't make sense to carry things that you can't turn over regularly in a short amount of time to keep things fresh.

Having said that, we also added a lot of items that we didn't think about before adding them to the menu. We tried to add items that other pizza shops didn't have just to be different.

Different isn't always better.

We would regularly add an item, not sell it, and end up removing it from our menu a month or two later. As soon as we removed it though, it seemed that's when customers wanted to order it.

Then there was the physical moving of our shop twice in our first six years. Each time we lost customers and had to almost start over.

When you move, even though you leave signs and advertise on your website, there will always be people who think you went out of business because you're not where you were before. The best advice here is, don't move unless it's next door or a few doors down where customers can still see you.

Lastly, in the inconsistency department, was hours. We changed our hours too many times.

There were times we wanted to capitalize on the late-night college crowd, so we would extend our hours to late into the night. It would catch up with us physically and we would cut back, sometimes drastically.

Then, some time would go by, and we would feel like we were missing too much business not being open later so we would extend our hours again. Back and forth we would go. Just pick the hours you know you can do and stick to them.

Customers aren't unreasonable. They want things to stay the same. That doesn't mean you can't put new things on a menu or add an hour to your hours of operation. It just means don't keep changing it.

Not Managing Our Building

This mistake was as big as any other and even though it has nothing to do with the business itself, it was perhaps the single biggest factor in our deciding to close.

Our building was a three-story brick building in the middle of the block downtown. The first floor was dedicated to our pizza shop and the basement was used for storage. The top two floors were apartments. They were 4-bedroom apartments that were in rough shape but were being rented when we first looked at the building.

We didn't want to be property owners and had the tenants removed before we closed on the building.

In hindsight, this was bad on several fronts. First, at $1,000 a month rent for each, that was a potential $24,000 a year that we were letting go. If you add up the entire time that we owned the building, that's about $300,000 in lost revenue.

Second, with no one living on the top floors, we didn't go up there much.

We had put a new roof on within the first year, so we didn't think we'd have a problem, but at some point, the roof had started leaking pretty badly. By the time we realized how bad things had gotten, the damage was done.

It was going to take a lot of money to fix what was going wrong and we had not saved up money, so we didn't have the means to make the repairs.

This was the final straw in our deciding to close.

If we had become property owners and worked on remodeling the apartments over time, we would have known right away about any leaks and would have had the money to make the repairs.

The lesson here is to take care of your property and check on things even when you don't think that you need to.

Safety Mistakes

I want to share a couple of stories with you about how being careless can have bad consequences. These are stories that really weren't about business specifically but rather things we did that caused problems that could have gone much worse.

The first one involves the back door. Just about everyone in the restaurant industry knows that you're supposed to keep the back door locked. You should, at the very least, keep it locked after dark.

Patti and I would usually split up our days. I'd come in early, and she would come in and cover lunch. We'd both be there for dinner. I would then go home just after dinner and come back around 10 p.m. or so to cover the late-night shift and close up.

One night, as I was returning to work, I saw two police cars with lights flashing parked out in front of our shop. I ran in to see what was going on.

A man had come into the shop and got a slice of pizza, looking to see how many people were working. At the time, it was Patti and one of our delivery drivers. Outside, the man waited and watched until the delivery driver left with an order. He then went around to the rear of the store and found the door unlocked, so he entered.

He grabbed Patti and dragged her up to the cash register and demanded that she give him all the money. Patti is a smart girl and told him to take it himself. That way fingerprints would be on the drawer. He grabbed the money and ran out the back door.

We were lucky. First, that Patti was unharmed. Second, that the police station was basically across the street, and it took them about three minutes to apprehend the thief after Patti quickly called 911 when the guy left. We were lucky, but this could have had a really bad outcome.

The second story involves a busy night that I ended up playing delivery guy because someone had called out and we were steady. I was in and out delivering all night. I would either park my car right in front of our store or in a parking spot that was in the alley right behind the shop to run in and grab two more deliveries before getting back out on the road. I would often not even turn off my car because I was always running right back out.

On one of these trips into the store, I ended up answering about three phone calls and waiting on a few take-out customers at the counter. I then picked up three orders for delivery and headed out the back door. My car wasn't there. I thought to myself, "Maybe I parked out front." I was pretty sure I didn't, and after passing through the pizzeria and out the front door to find there was no car there either, I knew the car had been stolen.

That was a bad night. I had to call the customers who had already ordered and explain that our delivery vehicle had been stolen. The previous day, I had been hit in the front of my vehicle, which smashed the driver's side headlight. When I spoke to the police, I told them that the car should be easy to spot at night since it only had one headlight.

Sure enough, the police caught the guy on the next night when he tried to drive around not knowing there was a light out. Unfortunately for me, I think the guy smoked about 50 packs of cigarettes while he drove my car. Other than that, I got it back unharmed. I should have never left my car unattended with the keys in the ignition. I was lucky again. These situations don't always have a good ending.

Chapter Two

Love at First Bite

I need to backtrack a bit and tell you how I ended up with a pizzeria. I didn't just wake up one day and decide I was going to get into the pizza business. There was a process. It started when my love for pizza and the accidental path into the restaurant business collided.

I still can remember discovering pizza. I knew then we were going to have a long, wonderful, relationship. I didn't know at the time just how big of a part it would play in my life, but I knew I loved pizza.

In 1969 my family moved to upstate New York from Lincoln, Nebraska. It wasn't long before somebody brought over some "Hot Pie." It was amazing. It had a crispy crust with perfect tomato sauce and gooey mozzarella cheese. It was so simple and yet so complex.

It would be a few years later though when I got hooked. I was 13 years old or so and had a paper route delivering the evening paper after school each day and the morning paper on the weekends.

One day, there was an insert in the paper for a new regional chain pizzeria that had just opened in our area. I had not tried it yet. The flyer had a coupon for two free slices of pizza, either plain cheese or with pepperoni, with a 12-ounce soda. Wow, what a deal!

I noticed that many of the papers had accidentally gotten two, three, or even five of the ad inserts in them. So, I figured it would be okay for me to snag the extras if everybody got at least one. By the end of my route, I had saved out around 30 of the extra inserts. Jackpot!

I was going to be able to eat pizza for free for the next 30 days. And I did. After I was out of coupons, I continued to go there regularly, spending some of my hard-earned paper route money.

At some point around that same time in my life, we started having Pizza Sundays at the house. It was our family day to make pizza together, whatever kind we wanted.

My father would go to a local bakery and purchase dough. He would bring it home and set the dough balls on the counter and cover them with moist cheese cloths to let them rise. When it was time, we would press them out onto oiled pans. Then we would sauce them with Ragu and put shredded mozzarella cheese on top. Toppings were put on last, on top of the cheese. The pepperoni was the favorite, but my parents liked to put on ground beef, onions, mushrooms, and extra cheese. I always looked forward to Sunday. It was a true family day. Everyone took part in making the pizzas. Then, of course, there was getting to eat the pizza we made. It was a perfect end to a great day.

About the time I turned sixteen, I started my first real job at a hardware store that was a few blocks from our house. I enjoyed the people I worked with and was starting to think about what I wanted to do with my life as far as a career was concerned. Working in a pizza shop was not part of my plan.

Entering the Restaurant Industry

I had decided that I wanted to become a sales rep for one of the hardware companies. A few years later when I started college, the courses I took were in business management with an emphasis on sales and marketing. I was also an avid bowler.

During my high school years, each day after finishing my paper route, I would head over to the bowling alley and bowl a few games. I got surprisingly good and at one point, thought I would like to turn pro and do that for a living (turns out, I wasn't that good).

One night, during one of the bowling leagues I was in, I met a team that included Burger King managers. That night after bowling, they invited me out for a beer. They were a lot of fun to hang out with, so I ended up going out with them regularly after bowling. When the season was over, they asked if I would be interested in joining their softball team.

Softball was a fun time, even though we lost most of the time. After each game, we would head over to somebody's house for an after-party. It was at one of these after-parties that one of the guys asked if would like to come work for him part-time to make some extra cash. I was going to college and paying my own way, so it was an easy decision.

About a week later I started my first job in a restaurant. I was 19 years old. A few weeks in I was hooked. I enjoyed the restaurant business a lot. I met my amazing wife there along with many other friends who I keep in touch with to this day. I stayed with Burger King for about seven years. When 1990 rolled around, I was bitten by the entrepreneur bug and decided I wanted to work for myself in the restaurant world.

A fast-food taco franchise was for sale in a small downtown mall. I made some inquiries, and after some negotiating, they hired me for a one-year deal with the option to buy at the end of the year. They were willing to hold a note on the business, so it seemed like a good deal to me. However, during that same year New York State enacted a law outlawing smoking in malls.

The small food court in this mall survived on the business from surrounding offices, but when the law went into effect, the smokers all migrated to the restaurants just outside the mall, where they could still smoke inside, taking their friends with them. It doomed the small food court.

At the end of the year, with the place struggling to make sales, I informed them that I was not going to buy the franchise. The next week, they closed it down. I felt like I had made a bad decision. I also didn't want to go running back to BK, even though I left on good terms. I decided that I would try something new.

For the next four years, I worked as a sales rep at a new car dealership. I enjoyed the interaction with customers, but something was missing.

My First Pizza Job

I started delivering pizzas for a local Domino's franchise and liked the business. I was a delivery driver; I never worked inside. Occasionally, I would make a pizza, but it wasn't what I did there. Still, somehow, I knew it was what I wanted to do.

In the back of my mind, I decided that I would look for a pizza shop.

Then one day in the summer of 1995, it happened. A realtor friend of mine called me up and said he was in a pizza shop earlier that day and had a conversation with the owner about selling.

The owner was an elderly Italian woman who had started the shop for one of her sons, but he wasn't interested in running a restaurant. At this point, she just wanted out. She wanted $14,000 for the equipment and said she would take payments on it over the next three years. To make things easier, my realtor friend said that he too would take his commission in payments. Patti and I talked it over and decided to take the plunge. Over the next couple of weeks, we scraped enough money together to make the first payments and buy our first order of supplies.

Here we were, about to open the doors to our first restaurant, and we had no idea what we were doing.

Patti was going to continue working at her job at a local credit union and I would start up the new pizzeria. Keep in mind that we had no YouTube or even internet for that matter to look up ideas or recipes. We started experimenting at home, eating pizza every night. Finally, the day came that it was time to open the doors.

Chapter Three

Freschott Pizza

We had decorated and cleaned for the two weeks leading up to our opening. We ate a lot of pizza and felt pretty good about our pie. We had a 30 qt. commercial mixer, but we had dough delivered each morning because we didn't know how to make it ourselves. We kept the phone number of the previous pizza place in hopes of getting some calls early on. We changed everything else, partly because the previous place didn't have a good reputation.

The name of our new baby was Freschott Pizza, pronounced "Fresh Hot Pizza," which posed its own problems, which I discussed in depth earlier.

We opened on August 14, 1995, and had a few calls the first night. We didn't know what to expect. I figured getting the place open and running would be the hard part. One thing I knew for sure though...I loved what we were doing. In our first week, I think we did about $700 in sales. They were long days. We opened at 11 a.m. and didn't close until 11 p.m. We were open seven days a week. We had five tables inside and a small take-out counter. There was dine-in, take-out, and we delivered.

In the beginning, it was me, Patti, and my father keeping the doors open. I opened the shop in the morning and my dad would come in for dinner. Patti would come down when she finished her day job. It was not very busy, so it was relatively easy to handle. We went on like that for a couple of months before we hired our first real employee.

*Me inside our first shop
in 1996.*

The Freschott Pizza exterior in 1995.

The Freschott Pizza interior in 1995.

The restaurant was growing in all our hearts. Patti and I were always working, which made it impossible to go to family events, so the family came to us. Our restaurant became the spot we would all gather for birthdays and other gatherings. My parents started a little tradition of showing up to eat on Friday nights. We would go out to the dining room and chat for a bit when we could. Other times when we were busy, they would just watch and smile. I miss those nights.

Some of my favorite memories include spending time with the family at the pizzeria.

During the first six months, we honed our pizza-making skills and upgraded our recipes on the fly. We ate a lot of pizza. I also began to read up on dough making and started the process of making our own dough. We changed the sauce three times in that first six months and each time it got a bit better (by the way, this is not a good idea. People like consistency).

We got lucky and the people who did notice, liked the improvements, and stuck with us. We also worked on our core menu. We added some specialty pizzas and sub sandwiches. Things really started to come together after the first year. Our menu was finalized, recipes were all worked out, and we had a few employees that worked out well.

Once we had that year under our belt, we felt like we were doing well enough that Patti could quit her job at the credit union and come to work at Freschott Pizza full time. We were not making boatloads of cash, but we were able to pay the bills and at least we were working for ourselves.

Through this experience, my passion began to really grow for the pizza business. I began to read books and trade magazines like *PMQ Pizza Magazine* and *Pizza Today* to learn as much as I could about this new life that we had adopted. I learned about dough, sauces, and different types of cheeses. I wanted to make a high-quality product. I wanted to run a great business.

Somewhere around the end of our first year, we realized that we really had an identity crisis. We had a small dining room with about six tables. We were trying to wait on tables and at the same time, with the same people, trying to handle take-out orders and deliveries. We just weren't big enough to do all of it effectively. I felt that we needed to make a decision on what type of shop we were going to be and focus on doing it right. We decided to be a take-out and delivery place with a few tables that people could eat at after placing their order at the counter. This helped us have better service and it was easier to take care of customers properly.

Things were going pretty good until our third year when we were forced to move at the end of our lease. It really caught us off guard. We began to look for a new spot and came across a location that had a Little Caesars that had just closed. The rent was quite a bit higher, but it was in a plaza that had a grocery store and several other businesses. We thought that would be a good place to move our baby and grow to the next level.

Growing Pains

The year was 1998. We had been in business for three years and were now being forced to relocate. We figured that since most of our business came from deliveries, customers would not care where we were delivering from as long as pizza showed up to their doorstep within half an hour.

The plaza that we moved to was only about a mile and a half away from our original location. The new spot was in a plaza that sat back from Main Street and slightly downhill. We thought it would be great.

Since we were moving, we thought that it would be a good time to sell some of our older equipment and upgrade to some more modern ovens. This was a mistake. We had to borrow more money to get them, and we didn't realize that they would not cook the pizza the same way.

It took us several months to figure out how to bake a pizza that we liked, and it was completely different than what we had been doing before. This time we were not so lucky. We lost customers and we were sick about it. It was too late now. We were all in. We bought radio ads, a huge yellow pages ad, and even did a TV commercial. It took a good year before we got things turned around and started making progress again.

When we finally got going with the plaza location, we thought we were doing it right. We invested quite a bit of money making it look like a place where you wanted to eat. We had a sign maker create a professional neon-lit sign that looked great. We had a pizza case for slices made to fit into our counter that held a dozen 16-inch pies so we could have a variety up at any given time. The concept, there, was to be a slice joint. We eventually knocked out a wall that went to our office and turned it into more dining area. We had it carpeted and bought a bunch of round tables that looked like pizzas.

We ordered new black metal chairs with black cushions to go with them. We were finally on track and making progress in sales.

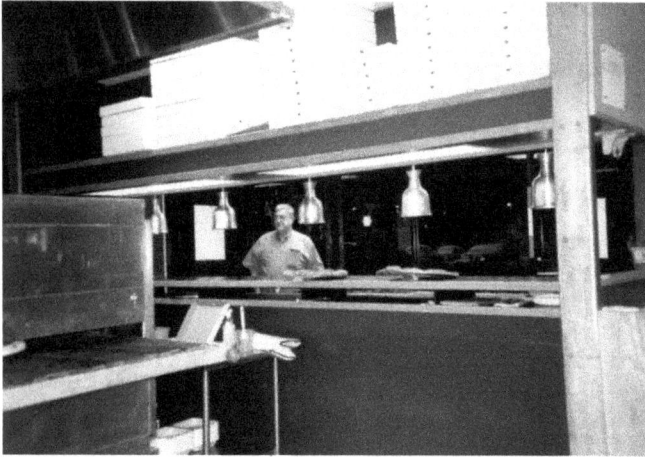

My dad inside our plaza location in 1998.

A Second Store

Toward the end of 1998, as we were getting back on track with our relocated store, an opportunity came up to purchase an existing pizza shop a couple of towns away from our current shop. We thought that it would be a good idea to have two stores that would be the same concept and would help us gain market share in both areas.

It was a deal that almost went sideways, but, in the end, worked out. When I answered the ad for a pizza shop for sale, I went to look at it and there wasn't much there. It had some old, partially working electric deck ovens, a household refrigerator, and a mop sink. There was also a marble-top pizza prep refrigeration unit that looked like it was on its last legs. The equipment wasn't great but was at least operable and we could get started and replace things as we went.

One night, a few days later, the guy who was selling it called me up and said he had to sell it quick, so he was willing to let it go for $2,500. I wrote him a check for a $300 deposit, and we were going to settle up in a couple of days.

However, the next day I got a call from the property owner telling me that the guy owed him a lot of money in back rent and that he had cut a deal with the guy to take equipment instead of payment. The seller had already skipped town with my deposit. The property owner was willing to give it to me for $1,500, so I made out better anyway.

We borrowed more money and upgraded some of the equipment at the new location. It was a low-budget operation that took us a few months to get better equipment. We bought a conveyor oven and hood, a three-door stainless cooler, and a refrigerated pizza make-line.

Things were going well at both stores. We continued to make improvements to the way we did things. We truly wanted to be the best at what we did, but we still had a lot to learn. Our menus were the same at both places and we did everything the same way at both shops. Patti ran the original store, and I took charge of the new one. We also had an assistant manager at each location. Things went well for quite a while, and we thought we were on track to continue growing.

Moving Again

That's when we found an old three-story brick building for sale in the heart of downtown Johnson City, New York. At the time, we had been in the plaza location for almost three years, and when it was time to renew the lease, we decided that the rent, which increased annually, was getting to be too much for us to be able to turn a profit. By purchasing the building, we'd no longer have to worry about leases or increasing rents.

After we purchased the building, we got to work transforming it into a pizzeria. We turned the first floor into our new pizza shop. It took us about three months of hard work. We took the plaster off the old walls to show off the original brick. We built a kitchen, bathroom, and a nice dining room complete with wooden booths that we built ourselves.

It was truly a labor of love. One Saturday when our new store was almost ready, we got a bunch of friends together and moved over all the equipment from the plaza location to the new spot. We got our health inspection on Monday and opened that same day in January of 2001.

The new store was exciting to open. We now had a place that we knew was ours for good and we built it from scratch.

The idea we had for the new place was to make it more of a sit-down restaurant. We had plenty of seating and had decorated each wall with its own theme. We had a movie- and TV-themed wall and a sports-themed wall. We put up three televisions to watch sports. We got a beer and wine license and began waiting on tables.

After a while, as with our first pizza shop, we realized that the sit-down model wasn't going to work for us in this location either. At one point, we even tried an all-you-can-eat lunch buffet. It did okay. Ultimately, we didn't do the kind of volume that it would take to keep the number of staff on, or to effectively take care of the dine-in, take-out, and delivery customers. So, we made some modifications to our counter area and returned to the counter service model.

Before long we built a regular lunch crowd with the tables filled for an hour or so every day during the week. Our other store was doing well, too. We ramped up our advertising and sales were growing.

Then it happened....

September 11, 2001

That morning, like every morning, I had pulled into my mother-in-law's driveway to pick her up and take her to work. She had been working in our pizza shop since the early days, making all our dough and doing a lot of the prep work.

When she came out to the car, she asked if I had heard about what was going on in New York City.

I had been listening to a CD in my car so didn't have it on live radio and had no idea what had happened. During our ride to work as I listened to the news, I got a sense that this was something really bad in ways we wouldn't know for some time to come.

It was scary.

I'm sure that almost everyone who is old enough to re-member knows where they were that day. And I know where they were not—in our dining rooms. I think that everyone was unable to leave their TV set that day. We were all glued to the screen in disbelief. What was going to happen next? For us, it was as if the whole town had disappeared.

Several days went by and still, people were staying in their offices or at home to track what was going on.

They never came back. Everything changed that day. Not just in the big picture of the world, but in our little piece of the pie.

I'll never know if there was more to it than that, but that's when things started to slide. A few months later, in March of 2002, we decided to close our second store. It wasn't growing and we thought we should focus all of our efforts on the building that we owned.

For a while, we continued to deliver to the area of our second store after we closed it. The business that came from that area slowly went away since we no longer had the store there.

Eventually, we cut off deliveries to the area and tried to get back to basics in our one remaining location.

The Next 10 Years

Time goes by so quickly. It seemed some days like we had just gotten into the pizza business, yet we had already moved twice, opened and closed a second store, and made so many changes that I can't even remember them all.

Over the next 10 years, from 2002 through 2012, we saw a lot of other pizza shops come and go. In the summer of 2006, we had three other pizza stores open within a 10-block radius of our store. One of them lasted about three months. Another didn't make it a full year. The third one is still there but has changed owners at least once.

We went up and down in sales over that time but were never able to pick up the steam that we wanted to be able to grow the pizzeria into something special.

We tried many different advertising avenues and had some successes. For example, around 2010, We began using a company called Mail Shark to manage our advertising. They are a company that designs, prints, and mails unique pieces made just for your pizzeria or restaurant. Each week they mailed out 1,000 pieces to carrier routes that were near our store. It worked great. Every week we knew we had a mailer going out and we just had to be ready for the sales.

That year turned out to be our busiest year and it had a lot to do with the program that Mail Shark put in place for us. A year later, they had a contest for testimonial videos. They would pick the best one and award a $500 prize. We sent in one that I did, and we won! However, we just couldn't leave well enough alone. Things were getting better, and we started making changes, many to the detriment of the business, which I discussed in earlier chapters.

Life Changes

In 2013, after having sales slide three years in a row from their all-time highs, Patti and I decided to make some drastic changes. Our building needed repairs that we didn't have money for, and our taxes were killing us. We had to get out. We decided to move south and get jobs. Even as I write this so many years later it still feels strange to say.

In November of 2013, I flew to North Carolina, in search of a new career. I returned home to New York a couple of days later with an offer to join Taco Bell as a general manager.

On January 1 of 2014 Patti and I packed our cars and drove down to our new apartment in Concord, North Carolina, where we had both taken jobs with Taco Bell. It was not easy leaving everything that we had built behind.

We had left the pizza shop open when we started off for our new life, but in February of 2014 we decided to close it, and that February 28 would be the last day. Patti and I were not able to be there for the closing, although I wish we were. We would have been able to say goodbye to the many customers who had become friends over the years.

It was a learning experience. They told me there would be a 6- to 8-week training period before taking over my Taco Bell store. I was thinking to myself, "Six to eight weeks? Really? Show me how to make tacos for a couple of days and give me the keys!"

After I started, I felt like I got punched in the head. I forgot what corporate restaurant work was like. There's a lot to learn, and everything has a specific procedure. I struggled a bit at first, but eventually got my bearings.

When I got to the store that would be mine, I had another week of training with the current manager of that store and then took a preplanned week-long vacation. When I came back from my vacation, ready to take over, half of the crew had quit because a new manager was coming in and they liked the old one.

I worked in that store for seven months before I was allowed to take on a busier store. The next store was a bigger project. It was short-staffed and was in a more difficult location to find good help.

I found myself working more hours than I could manage. My goal was to work as a GM for a year or two and then get promoted to area coach. However, with the hours I was working and the job itself requiring some very late nights, I wasn't happy where I was going and decided to make another change.

This time we moved north.

We didn't get all the way back home, but halfway there. I took a position with an Arby's franchisee in Southern Maryland as a district manager. I was to oversee four stores in the Virginia and Maryland market and would eventually add a fifth.

I jumped right into the work, helping to improve performance at each store. It took around six months to get them running on all cylinders. Stores that were losing money several months of the year were now profitable all 12 months. People working at the stores were happier and customers were getting better service.

Unfortunately for me, Arby's and the owner of our franchise had conflicting ideas about how things should be done.

I was on a cruise vacation when I got a text from our director of operations telling me that our franchise owner had sold his stores. We were told that nothing would happen to our jobs, but that was about as far from the truth as you could get.

Two weeks after the changeover, they told me that that day would be my last day.

I looked at a couple of options, but ultimately decided to return home. Patti and I would move in with my parents to help them and ourselves out.

What would we do for income? Open a pizza shop, of course.

Chapter Four

This Time... Let's Do It Right

Here we were, starting over. This was our chance to use the knowledge gained from the things we did right while avoiding the things that we did wrong. Would we pass the test in our new attempt at the pizza biz?

First, we had to have a plan about how we would do things. We needed to find a location to figure out what we had to work with and go from there. We knew we didn't want to go back to the area where we previously had a shop because it was one of the most depressed areas around. We also wanted to be relatively close to where we lived.

We finally settled on a location. It was previously an ice cream shop in the heart of Endwell, New York. It was a small free-standing building with plenty of parking. The rent was reasonable, and we were able to start working on it in the middle of June 2017.

Due to the size of the building, we only had enough room to be a take-out restaurant. There would be no room to put seating after we brought in the equipment we needed to operate. We decided that our menu would consist of pizza, sub sandwiches, calzones, and a few appetizers. We kept things simple. We had roughly 10 specialty pizzas, nine calzones, and about 20 sandwiches. Many of the ingredients crossed over to be used on several items to provide variety and keep the inventory costs down.

When it was time to come up with a name, we wanted a fresh start, so we didn't want to use the name of our old pizza shop. It needed to be a name people could pronounce and understand. We decided on Taylors' Neighborhood Pizza & Sandwich Shoppe. It's who we are and what we do. We made a neat little logo to go with it, too.

Our name and logo for the new pizza shop that opened in 2017.

Then we decided on hours that weren't going to wear us down. Closing at 8 p.m. Monday through Thursday, and 9 p.m. on Friday and Saturday. Closed on Sundays. That way we get time to recover even if we work every hour that we're open. We also wanted hours that could be stable. We didn't want to change hours all the time like we did with our first shop.

When everything else was ready to go, we brought the POS system in and got it set up to manage the new business. I had a friend tune it up before we got started, and everything worked as it should.

These computers and the software are about 12 years old now so we knew at some point, sooner than later, we would have to upgrade our systems. We've been using the Point of Success software for many years. When it was time to upgrade to the latest version, they gave us a great deal and helped us get everything set up.

Time To Open

Round two was beginning for us. August 21, 2017, we opened the doors to our new little shop. We did a bit of a soft opening. No fanfare. No advertising.

We put up our signage, turned on all the equipment and the open sign, and the new chapter began. People started coming in a little at a time. We are on a fairly busy road and just having the signs up gave us some decent exposure.

A couple of weeks in, we decided to send out some direct mail pieces. The response was good. We sent a postcard out to about 10 different carrier routes around the store. The postcard was simple and explained who we were and why people should check us out. We also made a conscious decision not to use coupons.

We make quality pizzas using fresh and unique ingredients. We bake the rolls for our subs, and our calzones are the perfect meal for one. Our philosophy is simple. We are a neighborhood pizza and sandwich place. We will get to know you.

We love to make our customers happy and have fun in the process. We have a 100% satisfaction guarantee, and we mean it. If someone is not completely happy with what they get, we will remake or replace their food or give them their money back.

The team knows that we all take care of our customers. They don't have to come running to me to handle an issue. They can fix it. I'm happy to say that we have only had to give money back twice since we opened in 2017. The main reason that we offer the guarantee is because we want customers to try new things without worrying that they spent money on something they might not like. It's how we can offer some unique items and get people to try them.

We've built a nice little business with plenty of room for growth. Our customers have done the bulk of our advertising. In our previous pizzeria, we spent a lot of money on advertising and put out a ton of coupons but just couldn't overcome the many mistakes that we made. This time we have built our business by making great food and giving customers an experience that keeps them coming back. Our team is strong, and we all have fun at work. It seems like every three to six weeks we are setting new records for sales. We still have a long way to go, but we are heading in the right direction.

Chapter Five

What Went Right

After embarrassing mistakes, missteps and moves, our pizza story could have ended, but it didn't.

Over nearly two decades in business, we had a lot of successes, too. And let me tell you, we learned from our mistakes.

So now I'll backtrack a bit and talk about what went right over the years.

These are the steps and promotions that worked to increase sales and grow customer counts. These are also the things that helped us stay in business for nearly 20 years. Besides, sharing what went right is more fun than talking about what went wrong.

Hopefully you can learn from my mistakes, use some of the things that worked, and grow your business to new heights.

Community Involvement

The more places that you represent your pizzeria to the community, the more opportunities there are for new customers to try your pizza and feel a sense of loyalty toward your shop. We would often get local groups coming in to solicit donations for various local functions. We didn't have to proactively go out and look for things to get involved in. However, I would highly suggest doing so.

Community involvement can come in many forms. There may be local government activities such as a Fourth of July fireworks display, a church function, such as a bazaar, or school activities, like sporting events.

Our best avenue was through the schools. One year, when someone inquired about donating a couple of pizzas to their after-prom party, I asked how many people they expected. She said they were going to have 250 and were just looking to have several pizza places donate a couple of pizzas each. I told her that I would be happy to donate all the pizza they needed if we were the only supplier. They agreed and we delivered all the pizza for them over the next 12 years. By doing that, we got a lot of publicity through the school and the parents of the kids that went to the party. After that, they started using us at their sporting events for concessions.

Our other regular involvement came from several local churches. We became known for our sheet pizzas that were cut into 24 square slices. They were perfect for selling at the weekly church bingo games to help with fundraising. At one time we were making the pizzas for four different church groups. These events usually had between 100 and 200 people each week, so a lot of people were getting to try our pizzas.

Another way to get yourself out in the community is through fundraisers. We were late to the game in this department, but when we did it, it had a big impact. Our radio sales rep asked if we would be interested in doing something for their local Christmas charity that bought toys for underprivileged children and delivered them during the holidays.

Sometimes they just put a drop box for new toys in your store or ask for pizza donations for the staff volunteering. This time I wanted to do more, so we ran a special for a week where we lowered the price of our large pizza by two dollars and then donated another two dollars to the charity to help buy gifts. It was truly a win-win-win promotion. Customers got a discount, the charity got money for gifts, and we got a lot of exposure to new customers.

Our rep was also the sales manager and she had me come down to the station to do a promo spot and an on-air interview about what we were doing. When the week started, I had no idea how hard it was going to be promoted. Wow! Those promo spots ran all day so many times I couldn't even count. The rep had gone out of her way to make it a huge success. At the end of the week, we were able to donate $1,000 to the charity and we had our busiest week in sales since we opened. What a great feeling it was to be that busy *and* to be helping kids in need.

Self-Promotion

In addition to being involved in your community, don't be shy about tooting your own horn to the local press.

In 1997, we were the first pizza shop in our area to offer online ordering. We contacted the local newspaper, and they came out and did an interview about the service.

I told them that I thought online ordering would be big and soon everyone would be doing it. To accompany the story, they took a photo of me pulling a fresh pizza out of the oven. Then, they put it on the front page of the paper. Boy, did we get some business from that. People would come in and say they saw the photo of our pizza and just had to come to try it out. You just can't buy that kind of advertising, and it was free!

Later that same year, we thought it would be a good idea to try and build on our success from the newspaper article by running a television ad. We had the station come down and film several clips at the shop. When the article in the paper came out, people loved the picture of the pizza coming out of the oven, so we made sure to incorporate that into our ads. We took several shots of us taking fresh pies out of the oven. The ad was a hit, and we were able to gauge the success by the numbers of new customers and by the people commenting when they came in that they thought the pizzas in the ad looked so good that they had to come in and try them.

We signed the contract for the ad in June. We set it up to run six times every Sunday between noon and 9 p.m. It was to begin in July and run through September of that year. The cool thing for us was that it carried us into football season on a station that carried NFL games. No one had realized that when they approved our contract, so we got the benefit of being on during games without the $300 each price tag that normally came with those spots. At the time we signed, I didn't even know that would happen, but we got a lot of exposure when it did.

The moral of the story is to find things that you're doing that no one else is doing and let people know about it. Many times, a local paper or TV station will pick up a local interest story and run it. This is the best kind of advertising that you can get. First, because it's free, but also because it's authentic. People love to see stories about local businesses that are impacting their community. Once a story is published, ride the wave of publicity with radio ads, flyers, and social posts.

Hiring A Good Staff

Over the years we had many great employees. Several were with us five to eight years at a time. We had some that went on to become doctors, lawyers, and even into the production side of television.

It takes all kinds of people to make a restaurant work. Many of the people who worked for us keep in touch today and are good friends.

We always tried to be good to our people. Through our time we took several of our crew on vacations with us to the Caribbean. Many of the people we had were more than just workers to us.

They were family.

What makes a good staff? I think that every employer is looking for the right team and life sure is easier when it's in place.

Everyone has different ideas about what the ideal employee looks like. There are some traits that I think most would agree should be part of what to look for.

They should, at first sight, be clean and presentable. We are in the food business. So, we want people who are clean handling our food. We started with people who were neat and clean and gave them a uniform and hat. We also had standards for what type of pants and shoes to wear. This way we ensured that people were presentable to customers whenever they worked.

Next, they need to be friendly. It's even better if they are friendly and outgoing. Everybody loves to see a smiley face. It makes you happy.

I look for people who smile when they talk to me and make eye contact. So many times, when you go into a restaurant, you're greeted by someone who has the personality of a gnat. You want to feel like they're glad that you came into their shop.

The other thing that I want to see is initiative. I want to have people who take it upon themselves to get things done.

It's our responsibility as employers to train people what to do, but it's much easier when you work with people who find things to do.

I want to run a pizza shop, not a daycare.

Door Hanging

Early on in our business, we employed the use of door hanging.

Door hanging is walking door to door throughout the neighborhood around the pizza shop and hanging a flyer or menu, often with coupons or limited time offers.

We found that we got a much better response rate when we included a menu with the flyer.

Door hanging is great because it's relatively inexpensive, targets a specific area near the shop, and frequently helps to get orders flowing in right away.

Afternoons were typically a slower time for us, so it made sense to send someone out to hang flyers during those hours.

We would usually have a local printer print about 1,000 flyers at a time, using the long half of legal-size card-stock paper. The printer also used a hole cutter to cut a one-and-a-half-inch hole at the top so we could hang the flyers on doorknobs and door handles.

The response rate for the flyers was typically 2% to 3%. That meant that every time we delivered 200 flyers, we would get four to six orders sometime shortly after they were delivered.

Sometimes, orders would come in up to two weeks later.

A routine of door hanging helped us get the word out and I would suggest this tactic for any pizza shop trying to let people know that it's open for business.

Direct Mail

For our mailings, we tried a couple of different methods. First, there's a program that you can do yourself through the post office called Every Door Direct Mail or EDDM. You sign up through the US Postal Service website and set up an account. They walk you through the process and it's pretty simple.

The EDDM program allows you to choose carrier routes around the store to mail to. There are usually around 500, plus or minus, to a route. There's also a lot of great demographic information available through the site. You can see which addresses are homes, apartments, or businesses. You can also see the average income and age demographics.

With EDDM, you must get the postcards or flyers printed and the postage insignia printed on the piece. Then you count and sort them into bundles of 50 or 100 and take them to an EDDM capable post office. Not all post offices can do them, so be sure to check before you get involved.

This is probably the cheapest form of mailing that you can do, but it does require some effort on your part to make it happen. The response rate for this type of direct mail fell between 2% and 3% for us.

In 2009, we got a flyer in the mail from a company called Mail Shark. In their ad, it said they had no upfront fees and there was an easy payment plan. What they do is a weekly mailing to carrier routes that you choose. They have an annual plan that mails out a piece for your shop for 50 out of 52 weeks of the year. They rotate between full-color menus, postcards, and magnet mailers. We talked it over and decided to try it.

It costs a bit more than doing the EDDM yourself, but they deliver professionally designed full-color pieces. As the mailers started hitting, we started to see an increase in sales. The program worked and we were seeing positive results.

The first piece to go out was a full menu. Sending a full menu got our name out there along with what we had to offer. There's also plenty of space for descriptions and pictures.

Then a postcard was mailed out to the same areas that the menus were sent to.

The third mailing was a magnet. The one we mailed featured the Monday night NFL schedule. This way, we figured it would make its way to the fridge if there were any football fans in the house. It would also help make an association between football and our pizza.

The fourth mailing was another menu and the fifth and final mailing of the year was a postcard.

Five times during the year we were hitting the same houses with fresh material, and each time the mailers went out, our response rate was 2% to 3%. Doing it this way helped to build sales in a compound way.

Each week more people were being retained as customers, compounding repeat business and sales.

The key to any advertising promotion is repetition, which we were able to achieve through mailer repetition. You have to get your name in front of people multiple times to get them to act.

POS System

We got our first point of sale (POS) system early on. Before getting it, we had been using paper forms that let you take up to 10 orders on each sheet. There were three parts to it. One part would go on a box, one part to a driver for keeping track of deliveries, and the last part stayed on the sheet to reconcile at the end of the day. It wasn't a terrible system, but it was cumbersome at the end of a shift. The POS made things so much easier and more accurate.

Just in mistakes prevented alone, I'm sure the POS saved us enough to pay for it in less than a year. No more spelling errors or wrong codes that created wrong pizzas being made. We also had a way to reconcile drivers at the end of the shift that was fast and correct. Having a POS gave us a way to track so many things. It was way more than just a cash register. We could track hourly sales, inventory, how many pizzas we were selling, and what toppings were the most popular. We weren't guessing anymore.

Having a POS system also gave us the ability to keep track of our customers. We could tell who was ordering and who was not. We could send out mail pieces to people who had not ordered in the last 60 days, for example. All of this helped with customer retention.

Pizza Cruises

That's right, I said pizza cruises. Patti and I, along with some of our friends, have been cruising together for years. In 2007, *PMQ Pizza Magazine* decided to sponsor its first Pizza Cruise. The idea was to gather pizza industry people from across the country and bring them together on a cruise vacation to share ideas and learn from each other while having the vacation of a lifetime. PMQ offered a few seminars put on by industry experts and held cocktail parties where we all got together and discussed the pizza business.

It was so refreshing to see that the pizza community was very willing to share ideas and experiences. I met several operators on the cruise and visited some of them in their shops after the cruise.

The whole experience gave me a sense of excitement that made me want to get back to my pizzeria and make things happen. It made me want to become a better operator.

We went on three of the four pizza cruises that PMQ organized, and if they ever start them back up, we'll be there, and would highly recommend them to others. It's great to be surrounded by people with the same passion for pizza and running their businesses.

Trade Shows and Competition

Trade shows are another place to be around some pretty amazing people in the pizza biz. Many of the pizzeria owners that attend and compete at these shows are well known in the business and are more than willing to help you out with just about anything. If you're having trouble with a recipe or need ideas on how to retain employees, these folks are always ready to talk with you and help find a solution.

The competitions at these shows are amazing. We competed for the first time in Milwaukee, in 2012. We met a lot of great people during that show. I was amazed how willing everyone was to share ideas, techniques, and honest discussions about problems they've had as well.

Chapter Six

What's Different Today?

A fter a break from the business, review of previous mistakes and successes, and a renewed mindset to start over, a lot is different today. I'm not only referring to my philosophy toward the business, but also how the general business climate has changed over the years.

No Coupons

First off, my philosophy on discounting has evolved. I'm not afraid to avoid coupons and specials. That's not to say that we won't run a special on something. When we do it though, it's on an item that we don't normally have, so there's no price comparison or expectation.

Today, we focus more of our time on food quality rather than speed and pick the best and freshest ingredients. I'm not saying that we didn't make good food in our last shop. We did. But with a focus on speed, we sometimes used pre-sliced meats, and bread that was delivered frozen, to save on prep time. Today, we bake our bread each day and slice meats and lettuce in-house. I want customers to taste the difference between us and other food places. There's passion in our food.

Using fresh ingredients has a cost. We price our products at a fair level and do not discount off of that. We let customers know that they are getting quality. Our prices are still in line with other places around us and, in most cases, better. We let customers know our philosophy, so they understand why we don't discount. I think many pizzerias across the country are held hostage by coupons. Many are afraid that if they don't offer deep discounts, people won't come in. That just isn't the case, but you must let people know what they're paying for.

Customer Service

The next part of my philosophy that has evolved over the years deals with how I approach and react to customers.

In the early days of our first business, I was so afraid that someone was going to trick me, that I listened to complaints with a grain of salt. Today, I believe that I truly understand customer service. Everyone is not out to scam me. If someone does, and I let them, chances are I will make that money back tenfold by treating the situation in a manner that turns them into a paying customer.

After working at some of the other fast-food chains, I observed how they were working to keep customers and it made sense. It's far less expensive to retain a customer than it is to find a new one. There are only three ways to raise sales: Get more customers. Get current customers to spend more each time they visit. Get current customers to come more frequently. That's it. Since two out of three of the possible ways to increase sales involve current customers, treat them like gold.

Any one of our team members has the authority to fix a customer service problem. By empowering the staff to fix things, they don't have to tell a customer to wait while they go get the manager. If there's a problem, fix it!

I don't care if it was the order taker's fault or the pizza maker or even the customer who made a mistake. I don't care; fix it! Have you ever walked into a restaurant with a problem and after you explain the issue, the staff starts to bicker about who did what wrong? That drives me crazy. It doesn't matter whose fault it is or who made what wrong. FIX IT! NOW!

A key element of what I wanted to accomplish with our new restaurant was to create a culture where everyone on the team understands real customer service. I want them to get to know their customers' names, what they like, and always greet them with a genuine smile. Everyone is important to the success of the company.

The Social Aspect

When we opened our first shop in 1995, we didn't even have the internet as we know it. So, the next big thing that's different today is that social media is a big part of the landscape. Now, not only is the internet everywhere, but every person is a potential food critic.

I've spoken with a lot of pizzeria operators and have listened to the various ways in which each deal with this new reality. I'm referring specifically to the handling of negative comments and reviews. People love to post everything these days, so if they have a bad experience, they let people know it in a very public way.

Some operators just ignore all the reviews. Some respond as though they are defending their honor and lash out at the posters. Then some respond to all with respect and address the concerns directly and try to come up with positive solutions.

I believe that positively responding to all is the best way to handle negative attention. It lets people know that you care about giving the customer a positive experience and that you listen to your customers. The hard part for a small business is staying on top of social media. Reviews and comments come from a myriad of sites from Facebook to Yelp and Google. It's practically a full-time job monitoring the different platforms.

Social media isn't all about the reviews, though. Many of these social media outlets can be a great way to get the word out about your shop. You can interact with your customers directly on many of these media. For example, on Facebook, you can set up a page for information about you and your shop with hours, menus, maps, and customers can ask questions or post their pics of your food. For business owners, there's also a way to boost your post and target specific customers around your shop. There are additional functions for getting people to apply for an open position at your shop.

The beauty of much of the social media attention is that you can reach a lot of people for free, or next to it. When customers leave positive reviews, other people take notice and many help spread the word when they like you and your products, and it costs you nothing. Be sure to use this to the best of your ability.

Sharing videos is one way I've differentiated us from our competition. I try to put out as much social media content as I can. Some weeks I put out a video each day and other weeks only once or twice. I always try to make the videos entertaining and informative.

Pizza Competitions

I decided that this time around I was going to get more involved in the pizza community. By that, I'm referring to the group of pizza operators that participate in culinary and acrobatic pizza competitions at trade shows. These people are great. There's such a vast knowledge of the pizza business from both the business side and the creative food side.

When I competed in Milwaukee in 2012, I was nervous cooking my pizza in front of people but met some good folks. This time around, my first competition was in Valley City, Ohio, in November of 2018. It was a US Pizza Cup event that had about 20 competitors from across the country. It was a real learning experience for me, and I made new friends that are always willing to share advice about pizza. I think I finished 16th in that first competition.

I competed in three events in 2019, including one at the end of the year in San Diego, California. It's been helpful to read the judges' comments after the competition to see where I can make improvements and hopefully do better the next time.

I've grown to love pizza competitions.

Spreading The Word

One of the advantages of competing is the press that it can generate. In 2019, after competing in Beltsville, Maryland, we were sent a press release from the US Pizza Cup about the event. I sent the release to all the local TV stations and the local paper. I heard back from the paper, and they wanted to do a story on us. Later that week, I heard from two of the television stations and they each wanted to come and interview us.

The TV stations aired their stories two nights apart that week and our sales went up, a lot. The reporter from the paper was going to come to do an interview the next week, but came out about three weeks later. I followed up each story with a Facebook post that had a link to the corresponding story. Our sales remain up almost 35% above where they were before all the attention.

As I mentioned before, this time we wanted to do things differently. That meant taking advantage of any opportunity that came our way. Always let people know when you do something positive that sparks interest or benefits the community, like fundraisers. It's imperative to the success of the pizza business to get recognition and food to as many people as possible. Get busy and get known!

Chapter Seven

The Pandemic

What do you do when the world turns upside down and everything changes?

Adapt.

We were on vacation, on a cruise, when we started to hear what was going on. Throughout our trip, everyone was talking about this thing called Covid. The cruise went out on February 29, 2020, and was one of the last ships to go out before things got crazy. Before we left, I didn't pay it a lot of attention. On our last port day before returning to the U.S., we were not allowed off the ship. Suddenly, we were no longer allowed to serve ourselves at the buffet, and the crew was constantly running around sanitizing everything. Previously, I had just assumed this was like when they hype the latest flu.

I was way off.

When we returned home around March 10, 2020, we started to hear a bunch of chatter about what was happening. I have friends in the pizza business all over the country and my phone was blowing up with all kinds of rumors and theories about what was yet to come.

One thing I knew was that people were starting to get scared.

Our customers were scared, too. You began to see it on the news every night. Stories of sickness and death spread across the world. Then came the masks and eventually shutdowns of dining rooms. In some places, the shutdowns were worse than others. Many restaurant operators could no longer use their indoor dining. It was going to be a rough go for many.

Here in our shop, we started to take some action right away. Since we're a take-out-only shop, we didn't have a dining room to close but made several adjustments to help make customers feel safe.

The first thing we did was lock our doors and only our team was allowed inside. We instructed customers to call when they arrived, and we would bring their food out to them. We took their payment info over the phone so there was no money changing hands. When the customer called and was in our parking lot, we would go out and place the order in a back seat or trunk so that there was no physical interaction between us and the customers.

Next, we had an app developed and sped up the process of getting online ordering for our shop. This made ordering a bit easier, especially during busy times when we had our phone lines tied up by customers calling to let us know they were here and ready for their orders.

We continued doing this for quite a while, until we started losing help. Finding people to work was going to be the next part of this crisis and still lingers on today. It became impossible to continue running orders out to cars when we no longer had enough team members to do so.

We decided to put up a large plexiglass shield between the customer area and the kitchen and counter area. This kept us isolated in the back. We had a schedule of wiping down and sanitizing all the counters, phones, door handles, etc. There was also a mask mandate in place so everyone in the store, both customers and staff, had to have a mask on in the store.

As time went on, the vaccine came out and people started to move about more freely. The mask mandate went away for vaccinated people and things have gotten as close to normal as they can, for now. We decided to leave the plexiglass barrier just to have a bit of perceived protection.

We were lucky in that we were already a take-out-only location. Many in our industry were not so lucky. They had to find ways that they were not used to, to be able to serve their customers.

I think it's important to keep all of this in mind when going forward with any restaurant project. This virus or another one could disrupt business as we know it at any time. We need to be able to pivot at any time. Keep that in mind when planning your take-out area. This pandemic has shown us a lot of things and we must learn from its lessons. We must always be able to adapt to the situation or the rules as they change.

We will succeed. Be there for your fellow operators. Help where you can. We are all going through some level of change. Learn from your peers. We will get through it.

Chapter Eight

Parting Advice

I f you've made it this far, thanks for sticking with me through all of the ups and downs of my pizza life story so far.

I'd like to leave some parting advice for anyone who may be considering joining the sometimes tough, but always exciting, pizza industry.

Have a basic plan. You don't necessarily need a full-blown business plan, but at least a good outline of what you want your business to look like. The more information that you can put together and the more details you have, the better your chances for success. Start with a statement about what you want to accomplish. Something like, "We are going to serve hand-crafted pizzas using locally sourced ingredients to residential customers in the Endicott community."

Decide on a menu. Knowing what you're going to serve will help you determine the equipment that you'll need. Knowing the equipment will help you determine the space needed. Everything goes hand in hand. The more you can decide and plan upfront, the more accurate you can be when it comes to setting up shop and making things go smoothly.

Plan your kitchen. Once you've decided on the type of restaurant, whether it will be a take-out; take-out and delivery; or full-service, then you can begin to layout the design for your kitchen. I believe that you always want to flow toward the customer. By that I mean that as you make the food, it should be working its way toward where the customer is in the shop. Have you ever noticed that when you go into a burger joint, as they make your food, it comes off the grill in the back, gets put together on a line in the middle, then gets put in a chute that slides up to the counter? This is what I'm referring to. You can stretch out the dough in the back, then pass it up to a make line for sauce, cheese, and toppings. After that, it moves into the oven, which is a little closer to the counter, and finally, to a cut table where it's put on a pan or in a box and given to the customer. Have the layout make sense from an efficiency standpoint.

Find your spot. Choosing a location is one of the most important decisions you will make. Be sure to keep a few things in mind when looking for your location. As I mentioned earlier, make sure the spot can accommodate your needed equipment. In addition, make sure the location is visible, with easy-in and easy-out parking that's ample for the number of customers that you plan to serve (for example, a parking spot for every two seats is a good rule of thumb). Other considerations include demographics around the location and room for expansion, should that be a need in the future.

Meet with local planning and health departments. Before any project can get started, you will likely have to get approval from a local planning board or committee. Some codes must be followed along with zoning that sometimes requires a special use permit or variance to operate a restaurant. They will walk you through the process and will also help make sure you know what to expect. Health departments may also require you to submit plans to them for approval before you start. You don't want to build something only to find out you have to take it apart and do it differently. In general, it's wise to be proactive and go to them to make sure your project gets off on the right foot.

Find dependable contractors. You will likely have to do some work to make the spot your own. Unless everything is already there, you will have plumbing, electrical, and maybe some construction. Look for people who you can trust to be there when you need them and that charge reasonable rates for the work to be done. It's a good idea to have these folks on speed dial anyway, as you never know when issues may arise. Talking with others you know in the business can help you find the right people.

Source your products. Look for a couple of food and paper goods vendors that can supply you with the products and ingredients that you will be using in your new restaurant. I have always used two vendors. Using only one vendor can leave you scrambling if they short you on a key ingredient. Using two vendors lets you compare pricing and keep them honest if they want to keep your business. If you try to use more than two vendors, it may be difficult to meet all the minimum order requirements to keep them. When deciding between vendors, make sure they carry your main product brands, so you don't have to substitute your core products, and ask if their trucks are in your area more than once a week in case you forget something or are busier and need an extra delivery.

Hire your staff. This is the one that could make or break you. Having the right people around you will help make your business run smoothly and your life will be easier. Hiring the wrong people will leave you working 80 hours a week with a stress level that's through the roof. Try to gather as many applications as possible. There are several places where you can advertise for free to obtain applications. Be sure to put a description in your ad that sets the qualifications you want in your candidates. Today, sadly, it's very common that people don't even show up for interviews. I've found that I have a better chance of them showing up if I call and talk to them first. Planning interviews online with no voice communications is practically a guarantee that they won't show up for their interview. Another way to get potential workers is to hold a hiring day or open interview day. Talk about it on social media and get people excited about your opening and let them know you're hiring on the spot on your open interview day.

Open your new shop. You've done the planning. You found the perfect spot. You built an efficient kitchen. You passed all your inspections and have your permits in hand. You hired the right staff and now you're ready to go. At this point, I like to do a "soft opening." This is where you invite friends and family and workers' families to come and try out the restaurant. You can also let in a few others if you want. This lets you see how it all works in a live setting without getting too busy before you're truly ready. It lets you work out any bugs in the system and fix any potential problems. Once you're sure you're all ready to go, open the doors and start your success. Have fun! Down the road, when you're running on all cylinders, be sure to plan a grand opening to get the buzz going about your new place.

Chapter Nine

What's Next?

S o, what do we do now that we have a successful little shop? Keep it going!

We will continue to do the things that have gotten us where we are today. We make consistently good food and give great customer service. Our feature pizzas have become a fun and rewarding part of our growth. I will also continue to compete in events and learn from my pizza brothers and sisters from around the world.

But there's more. We recently found another location, a few doors down from our current spot, where we can add seating and craft beer to our enterprise.

I have always maintained that craft beer and craft pizzas belong together. It's an exciting journey that we are on and can't wait to get to the level where we can make it all happen.

Stay tuned for our next adventure. So far this has been a rollercoaster ride that has had many ups, downs, and turns. And like most rollercoaster rides, I'm ready to go again.

Recommended Reading

There are many books about pizza and the industry, but these are a select few that I encourage you to read. There's a lot of information and stories in these that make them a go-to source for people wanting to learn and grow in the pizza business.

- *Marketing from the Trenches: Your Guide to Retail Success* by Rudolf J Waldner
- *The Pizza Equation* by Nick Bogacz
- *The Pizza Bible* by Tony Gemignani
- *Pizza: A Slice of American History* by Liz Barrett
- *The Guerilla Marketing Handbook* by Jay Conrad Levinson and Seth Godin
- *Profits in the Pie* by Scott Anthony
- *Unsliced* by Mike Bausch

Let's Stay in Touch

I plan to start talking to other operators about their life experiences in the industry and get those interviews shared.

It's always been a goal of mine to hear the stories behind other pizzerias. There are many great people in the business, and I want to share them all with you.

We will focus on the personal side of things—where the owners came from and how pizza selected them as ambassadors. It will be fun and informative.

Thank you for sharing A Pizza My Life!

Let's Stay in Touch!

You can reach me at george@taylorspizza.com.

About the Author

George D. Taylor has been in the pizza business for 25 years. He and his wife Patti currently own Taylors' Neighborhood Pizza & Sandwich Shoppe in Endwell, New York, which they began in 2017. Taylors is a family-run take-out pizzeria that specializes in delicious, made-to-order pizzas, slices, and monthly pizza and sub sandwich specials that use the finest ingredients available. George is a regular competitor at culinary pizza competitions around the country where he benefits from the competitive spirit and pizza industry camaraderie. Find out more about George and the pizzeria at www.taylorspizza.com.

www.ingramcontent.com/pod-product-compliance
Lightning Source LLC
Chambersburg PA
CBHW060622200326

41521CB00007B/858